Rūfus et arma ātra

a Latin Novella
by Lance Piantaggini

Poētulus Publishing
magisterp.com

Index Capitulōrum
(et Cētera)

Praefātiō

Following the success of *Pīsō Ille Poētulus*, this spin-off novella focusing on Piso's younger brother is the latest to address the lack of understandable reading material with sheltered (i.e. limited) vocabulary available to beginning Latin students.

Rūfus is written for the true novice, able to be read within the first year, and likely within the first few months of school! *Rūfus* contains just 40 unique words (excluding names, different forms of words, and meaning established within the text). A closer look at obvious cognates (e.g. *exspectat, gladiātor, ineptus, īrātus, optimus, sordidus, etc.*), other likely recognizable derivatives (e.g. *frāter, multa, etc.*), and frequent conjunctions, prepositions, and adverbs (e.g. *ad, ē/ex, et, iam, in, nōn, quoque, sed, etc.*) would lower the count to under 25! *Rūfus* has the lowest unique word count of all currently published Latin and modern language novellas.

The *Index Verbōrum* is rather comprehensive, with an English equivalent and example phrases from the text found under each vocabulary word. Meaning is established for every single word form in this novella.

I thank members of the Latin Best Practices group for reading *Rūfus* with their classes, as well as the Latin students of Amherst-Pelham Regional High School for their input. Lauren Aczon's illustrations provide significant comprehension support for the novice reading *Rūfus*. See more of Lauren's artwork on Instagram @leaczon, and/or on her blog, (www.quickeningforce.blogspot.com).

Magister P[iantaggini]
Northampton, MA
March 1, 2017

I
Rūfus

est Rūfus.
gladiātōrēs eī placent.

eī placent gladiātōrēs magnī.
eī placent gladiātōrēs parvī.

Rūfus

bonī gladiātōrēs eī placent,
et malī gladiātōrēs eī quoque placent!

gladiātōrēs eī valdē placent!

gladiātōrēs pugnant.[1] Rūfus quoque pugnat, sed gladiātor nōn est.

Rūfus frātrem habet.
frāter est Pīsō.

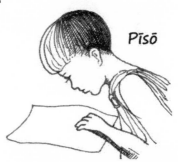

Pīsō

Rūfus in frātrem,
Pīsōnem, pugnat!

multa arma

gladiātōrēs multa
arma habent.

ergō, arma Rūfō
quoque placent.

---

[1] **pugnant** *fight*

7

Rūfō placent arma magna.

Rūfō placent arma parva.

arma mala!

bona arma eī placent, et mala arma eī quoque placent!

Rūfō gladiātōrēs et arma valdē placent!

Rūfus est Rōmae.[2]

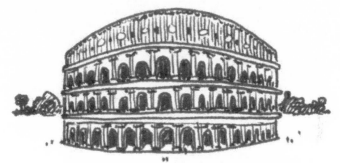

Amphitheātrum Flāvium

gladiātōrēs in Amphitheātrō Flāviō[3] pugnant Rōmae.

est diēs Veneris.

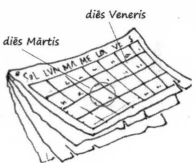

diēs Veneris

diēs Mārtis

diē Mārtis,[4] gladiātōrēs in Amphitheātrō Flāviō pugnābunt.

---

[2] **Rōmae** *in Rome*
[3] **in Amphitheātrō Flāviō** *in the Colosseum*
[4] **diē Mārtis** *on the day of Mars (i.e. on Tuesday)*

diē Mārtis, pugna bona erit. diē Mārtis, Rūfus laetus erit!

Rūfus diem Mārtis exspectat. Rūfus pugnam bonam in Amphitheātrō Flāviō exspectat.

Rūfus exspectat et exspectat et exspectat...

II
Rūfus et frāter

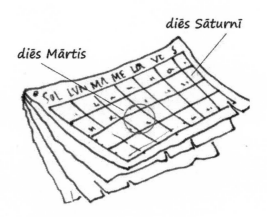

diēs Sāturnī

diēs Mārtis

iam, est diēs Sāturnī. Rūfus pugnam bonam diē Mārtis exspectat. pugna bona in Amphitheātrō Flāviō erit.

Rūfus:
"Pīsō, diēs Sāturnī est.
vīsne īre ad
Amphitheātrum
Flāvium diē Mārtis?"

Pīsō:
"īre ad
Amphitheātrum
Flāvium mihi
nōn placet."

Pīsōnī gladiātōrēs nōn placent.
Pīsōnī arma nōn placent.

ergō, Pīsō ad Amphitheātrum Flāvium
nōn it.

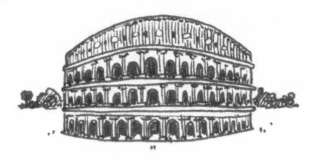

Rūfus:
"diē Mārtis ad Amphitheātrum Flāvium
īre volō. gladiātor optimus pugnābit!
laetus erō!"

Pīsō:
"Rūfe, īre ad Amphitheātrum Flāvium
NŌN MIHI PLACET!"

Rūfus:
"male olēs,[1] Pīsō!"

Pīsō:
"nōn male oleō!
MALE OLĒS, RŪFE!"

Rūfus īrātus est, sed pugnam in Amphitheātrō Flāviō exspectat. diē Mārtis Rūfus laetus erit.

Rūfus exspectat et exspectat et exspectat...

---

[1] **male olēs** *you smell bad*

III
Amphitheātrum Flāvium

diēs Mārtis

Rūfus diem Mārtis exspectābat.
iam, est diēs Mārtis!

est pugna bona Rōmae. pugna bona est in Amphitheātrō Flāviō. gladiātōrēs in Amphitheātrō Flāviō iam pugnābunt!

Rūfus laetus est!

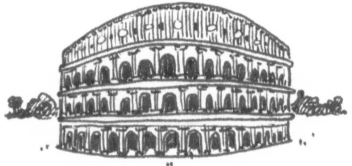

Rūfus ad Amphitheātrum Flāvium it. frātrī, Pīsōnī, gladiātōrēs nōn placent. ergō, Pīsō ad Amphitheātrum Flāvium nōn it.

Rūfus in Amphitheātrum Flāvium it.
iam, Rūfus in Amphitheātrō Flāviō est.

in Amphitheātrō Flāviō, sunt multī
gladiātōrēs!

 gladiātōrēs arma
multa habent.

gladiātōrēs gladiōs parvōs habent.

gladiātōrēs gladiōs magnōs habent.

 gladiātōrēs habent
scūta parva...

...et gladiātōrēs habent scūta magna!

Rūfō arma placent.
ergō, Rūfus laetus est.

in Amphitheātrō Flāviō,
multī gladiātōrēs iam pugnant.

aliī[1] gladiātōrēs bene…aliī gladiātōrēs male pugnant.

gladiātor ineptus in gladiātōrem alium cadit[2]—super alium alius![3]

---

[1] **aliī…aliī…** *some…others…*
[2] **cadit** *falls*
[3] **super alium alius** *one after the other*

gladiātor ineptus male pugnat.
Rōmānī gladiātōrem optimum
exspectant.

subitō, in Amphitheātrum Flāvium
gladiātor optimus, Crixaflamma, it!

21

IV
pugna

Rōmānī:

"Crixaflamma! Crixaflamma!
Crixaflamma!"

Crixaflamma est gladiātor optimus. Crixaflamma bene pugnat.

arma

aliī gladiātōrēs[1] arma habent, sed Crixaflamma arma ātra habet.

Crixaflamma gladium ātrum et magnum habet. Crixaflamma scūtum ātrum et magnum quoque habet.

arma ātra

---

[1] **aliī gladiātōrēs** *the other gladiators*

arma ātra optima sunt! arma Rūfō placent, sed arma ātra eī valdē placent!

Crixaflamma habet
lanistam[2] optimum.

est Oenobatiātus.

Oenobatiātus:
"pugnā, Crixaflamma, pugnā!"

---

[2] **habet lanistam** *has a gladiator trainer*

iam gladiātōrēs pugnant!

sunt gladiātor optimus, Crixaflamma, et nēsciō-quis[3] gladiātor malus.

Crixaflamma arma ātra optima et magna habet.

---

[3] **nēsciō-quis** *I-don't-know-who (i.e. Mr. no-name)*

gladiātor malus gladium parvum et scūtum parvissimum[4] habet.

Crixaflamma in gladiātōrem malum pugnat!

gladiātor malus gladium parvum ad scūtum Crixaflammae iacit. scūtum Crixaflammae optimum est.

---

[4] The more common word for "really small" is *minimum*, but the ancient authors Lucretius and Varro also used *parvissimum*. You could think of it as sounding a little silly, perhaps meaning something like "itty-bitty."

gladiātor malus gladium iam nōn habet!
Crixaflamma laetus est.

gladiātor malus scūtum parvissimum
iacit ad Crixaflammam.

gladiātor malus est ineptus!
gladiātor malus cadit—in scūtum cadit!

gladiātor malus super scūtum iam est. gladiātor malus īrātus est. gladiātor malus et ineptus et īrātus gladium iam quaerit.[5]

Crixaflamma gladiātōrem malum exspectat...

---

[5] **quaerit** *searches for*

iam, Crixaflamma gladiātōrem malum iacit!

gladiātor malus laetus nōn est.

Rūfus:
"Crixaflamma
nēsciō-quem
gladiātōrem
malum iēcit!"

Crixaflamma gladiātōrem malum
in gladiātōrem alium iacit!

gladiātōrēs cadunt—super alium alius!
Crixaflamma pugnat et pugnat et
pugnat. Crixaflamma gladiātōrēs malōs
et ineptōs iacit et iacit et iacit.

Rōmānī:
"Crixaflamma
optimus est!
optimus est
Crixaflamma!
optimus Crixaflamma est!"

Oenobatiātus:
"Crixaflamma est optimus! lanista optimus sum!"

Crixaflamma laetus est. Oenobatiātus laetus est. Rūfus laetus quoque est.

Rōmānī laetī sunt!

V
arma Crixaflammae

Crixaflamma ex Amphitheātrō Flāviō it. lanista, Oenobatiātus, et gladiātōrēs bonī ex Amphitheātrō Flāviō quoque eunt, sed laetī nōn sunt.

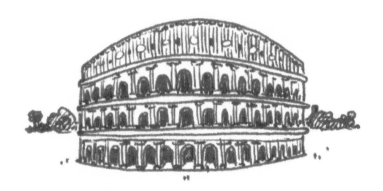

Rūfus:
"Crixaflamma, es gladiātor optimus! arma ātra mihi valdē placent, sed...sed... sed—Ubi sunt arma?"

Crixaflamma:
"arma ātra optima erant in Amphitheātrō Flāviō, sed iam in Amphitheātrō Flāviō nōn sunt! arma iam nōn habeō!"

Rūfus:
"Quis arma ātra habet?"

Crixaflamma:
"nēsciō! lanista,
Oenobatiātus,
īrātus est.
Quōmodō pugnem?!"[1]

---

[1] **Quōmodō pugnem?!** *How am I supposed to fight?*

Rūfus iam nōn est laetus. Crixaflamma arma habēbat, sed arma iam nōn habet! Crixaflamma arma vult. Rūfus vult Crixaflammam esse laetum.[2] ergō, Rūfus arma quoque vult.

Rūfus:
"arma ātra quoque volō.
arma quaeram!"

> *Crixaflamma:*
> "bonus es, sed—Quis es?"

Rūfus:
"sum Rūfus. amīcus sum."

> *Crixaflamma:*
> "optimē, Rūfe! arma quaerāmus!"[3]

---

[2] **vult Crixaflammam esse laetum**
   wants Crixaflamma to be happy
[3] **arma quaerāmus!** *Let's search for the weapons!*

Oenobatiātus:
"laetus nōōōōōn sum!
īrāāāāāāāāāātus sum.
īrāāāāātissimus sum!
UBI   SUNT   ARMA?!
QUIS HABET ARMA?!"

gladiātōrēs bonī:
"Oenobatiāte, nēscīmus!"

Oenobatiātus:
"gladiātōrēs, arma quaerite!
īte ad Cloācam Maximam![4]
īte ad lūdum![5]
ARMA ĀTRA QUAERITE!"

---

[4] **īte ad Cloācam Maximam!** *Go to Rome's sewer!*
[5] **īte ad lūdum!** *Go to the gladiator school!*

aliī gladiātōrēs in
Cloācā Maximā...

...aliī gladiātōrēs in lūdō lanistae,
Oenobatiātī, arma ātra quaerunt.

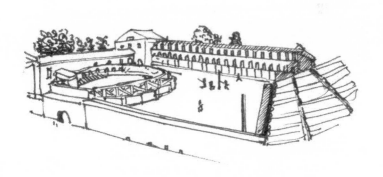

Rūfus arma ātra quoque quaerit,
sed nōn quaerit in Cloācā Maximā!

Rūfus:
"euntne gladiātōrēs
ad Cloācam Maximam?
fūfae!"[6]

---

[6] **fūfae!** *Gross!*

VI
Rūfus et arma ātra

Crixaflamma arma ātra vult.

Crixaflamma laetus nōn est. Rūfus vult
Crixaflammam esse laetum. ergō, Rūfus
arma ātra quaerit.

Rūfus:
"Quis habet arma ātra Crixaflammae?
Ubi sunt arma? suntne arma in Forō
Rōmānō?"

Forum Rōmānum

Rūfus ad Forum Rōmānum it. multī Rōmānī in Forō sunt, sed arma in Forō nōn sunt.

Rūfus:
"Ubi sunt arma Crixaflammae? suntne arma in Circō Maximō?"

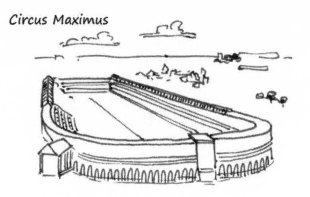
Circus Maximus

Rūfus ad Circum Maximum it.

subitō, gladiātōrēs
ē Cloācā Maximā
cadunt!

gladiātōrēs sordidī[1] sunt!
gladiātōrēs arma ātra nōn habent.

---

[1] **sordidī** *dirty*

gladiātor sordidus:
"nōn sunt arma ātra in Cloācā Maximā.
Cloāca Maxima sordida est."

Rūfus:
"gladiātor,
sordidus ES—fūfae!"

subitō, Oenobatiātus ē Circō Maximō it!
Oenobatiātus cadit. Oenobatiātus est
īrātus.

Oenobatiātus:
"sunt arma
in Circō Maximō, sed
arma nōn sunt ātra.
UBI SUNT ARMA?!
Quis—Quis male olet?"

Rūfus:
"gladiātōrēs male olent!
gladiātōrēs in Cloācā Maximā erant.
gladiātōrēs sordidī sunt!"

gladiātōrēs bonī:
"sordidī sumus.
male olēmus."

Oenobatiātus:
"fūfae! sed—UBI SUNT ARMA ĀTRA?!"

gladiātor sordidus:
"Oenobatiāte,
gladiātōrēs aliī
ad lūdum ībant."

Oenobatiātus:
"suntne arma in lūdō?
ad lūdum eāmus!"[2]

---

[2] **eāmus!** *Let's go!*

subitō, Pīsō ad Rūfum it!

Rūfus:
"Pīsō, Crixaflamma arma
ātra optima nōn habet!
arma ātra in Forō Rōmānō
nōn sunt...in Cloācā
Maximā nōn sunt...
in Circō Maximō nōn sunt!
vīsne arma quaerere
in lūdō lanistae, Oenobatiātī?"

Pīsō:
"Rūfe, arma
mihi nōn placent.
arma nōn quaeram.
ad Forum Rōmānum eō."

Rūfus:
"sum amīcus Crixaflammae.
arma quaeram. arma volō!
arrrrrma volōōōōō!"

Pīsō:
"ARMA NŌN
QUAERAM, RŪFE!
quaere arma in...in...
in lūdō nēsciō-cūius lanistae malī!"[3]

suntne arma ātra in lūdō lanistae malī?
ad lūdum lanistae malī Rūfus it.

---

[3] **in lūdō nēsciō-cūius lanistae malī**
  in I-don't-know-whose gladiator school
  (i.e. in the gladiator school of Mr. no-name)

VII
lūdus lanistae malī

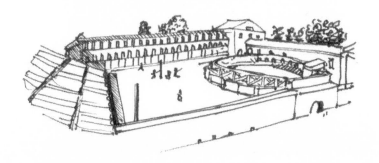

Rūfus in lūdō est. lūdus malus est, et male olet. est lūdus lanistae malī, nōn est lūdus optimus Oenobatiātī. lūdus Oenobatiātī bene olet—nōn male olet! lūdus Oenobatiātī nōn est Rōmae.

iam, Rūfus est Rōmae in lūdō malō nēsciō-cūius lanistae malī.

sunt multī gladiātōrēs in lūdō malō.
gladiātōrēs pugnant, sed male pugnant.
gladiātōrēs nōn bonī sunt—gladiātōrēs
malī sunt!

gladiātor
ineptus cadit.

gladiātor ineptior in gladiātōrem malum
cadit—super alium alius!

gladiātor ineptissimus
in gladium cadit!

gladiātor ineptissimus laetus nōn est.

in lūdō malō sunt arma multa. alia arma
magna...alia arma parva sunt. alia arma
bona...alia arma mala sunt. suntne arma
ātra Crixaflammae in lūdō malō? Rūfus
exspectat.

subitō, lanista malus in lūdum it!

Rūfus:
"est nēsciō-quis lanista malus!"

lanista malus:
"laetus sum! arma ātra Crixaflammae
iam habeō! Crixaflamma gladium et
scūtum nōn habet. iam Crixaflamma
optimus gladiātor nōn est!"

Rūfus est īrātus. lanista malus habet
arma ātra Crixaflammae! Rūfus arma
vult. Rūfus lanistam malum iacere vult![1]
Rūfus ad lanistam malum iam it.

Rūfus:
"lanista male, habēs arma ātra optima
Crixaflammae! Crixaflamma gladiātor
optimus est. es malus lanista.
arma ātra volō!"

---

[1] **iacere vult** *wants to throw*

lanista malus iam īrātissimus est. lanista malus vult iacere Rūfum! lanista malus ad Rūfum iam it.

subitō, Oenobatiātus, in lūdum malum it!

Oenobatiātus:
"Crixaflamma, pugnā!"

subitō, Crixaflamma in lūdum malum quoque it!

Crixaflamma arma nōn habet, sed in gladiātōrēs multōs pugnat!

Crixaflamma gladiātōrem īrātum iacit in gladiātōrem alium. gladiātor alius īrātior cadit in gladiātōrem īrātissimum! gladiātōrēs malī et ineptī sunt!

Crixaflamma pugnat et pugnat et pugnat. Crixaflamma gladiātōrēs multōs iacit et iacit et iacit. gladiātōrēs cadunt et cadunt et cadunt.

iam, Crixaflamma in lanistam malum pugnat. Crixaflamma lanistam malum iacit!

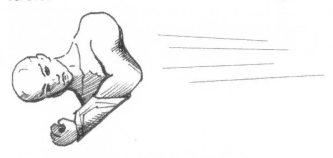

lanista malus nōn est laetus.

lanista malus ad Crixaflammam it, sed cadit. lanista malus īrātissimus est!

Crixaflamma exspectat. Oenobatiātus exspectat. Rūfus quoque exspectat.

subitō, lanista malus arma ātra iacit!

lanista malus:
"Crixaflamma, es
gladiātor optimus.
sum lanista malus...
et...et...et ineptus.
habē[2] gladium ātrum!
habē scūtum ātrum!"

Rūfus:
"...et lūdus malus?
volō Oenobatiātum
habēre[3] lūdum."

lanista malus:
"Oenobatiāte, es lanista optimus.
habē quoque lūdum!"

---

[2] **habē!** *Have!*
[3] **volō Oenobatiātum habēre** *I want Oenobatiātus
to have*

Oenobatiātus:
"optimē! iacite lanistam
malum et gladiātōrēs
malōs et ineptōs
in Cloācam Maximam!"

Rūfus et Oenobatiātus et Crixaflamma lanistam malum et gladiātōrēs malōs ē lūdō et in Cloācam Maximam iaciunt! fūfae!

Oenobatiātus lūdum lanistae malī iam habet. Crixaflamma arma ātra iam habet.

ergō, Oenobatiātus et Crixaflamma laetī sunt. Rūfus quoque laetus est.

Crixaflamma:
"es bonus, Rūfe.
parvus, sed bonus es.
es amīcus bonus."

Rūfus:
"...et...et nōn male oleō!"

Crixaflamma:
"optimē, Rūfe!
et nōn male olēs!"

Index Verbōrum

A, B

ad *to (toward)*
    īre ad *to go to*
    iacit ad *throws towards*

alia *some, others*
    alia...alia... *some...others...*
    alia arma *some weapons*

  aliī *some, others*
    aliī...aliī... *some...others...*
    aliī gladiātōrēs *other gladiators*

  alium *another*
    in gladiātōrem alium *into another gladiator*
    super alium alius *one after another*

  alius *other, another*
    super alium alius *one after another*
    gladiātor alius *another gladiator*

amīcus *friend*
    amīcus esse *to be a friend*

Amphitheātrō Flāviō *Flavian Amphitheater (the Colosseum)*
    in Amphitheātrō Flāviō pugnāre *to fight in the Colosseum*
    ex Amphitheātrō Flāviō esse *to be outside of the Colosseum*

  Amphitheātrum Flāvium *the Colosseum*
    īre ad Amphitheātrum Flāvium *to go to the Colosseum*
    in Amphitheātrum Flāvium *into the Colosseum*

arma *weapons, armor*
    arma habēre *to have weapons*
    arma placēre *to like weapons*
    arma quaerere *to search for weapons*
    arma iacit *throws weapons*

ātra *black*
    arma ātra *black weapons*

  ātrum *black*
    gladium ātrum *black sword*

bene *well*
    bene pugnant *fight well*
    bene olet *smells good*

bona *good (more than one)*

bona arma *good weapons*
bonam *good*
pugnam bonam *good fight*
bonī *good (more than one)*
bonī gladiātōrēs *good gladiators*
bonus *good*
bonus es *you are good*

C, D

<u>**cadit**</u> *falls*
cadit in *falls into*
in scūtum cadit *falls onto a shield*
Oenobatiātus cadit *Oenobatiatus falls*
gladiātor ineptus cadit *a clumsy gladiator falls*
cadunt *(more than one) fall*
gladiātōrēs cadunt *the gladiators fall*
ē Cloācā Maximā cadunt *they fall out of Rome's sewer*
<u>**Circō Maximō**</u> *Circus Maximus*
in Circō Maximō esse *to be in the Circus Maximus*
ē Circō Maximō it *goes out of the Circus Maximus*
Circum Maximum *Circus Maximus*
ad Circum Maximum it *goes to the Circus Maximus*
<u>**Cloācā Maximā**</u> *Cloaca Maxima, Rome's sewer*
in Cloācā Maximā quaerunt *they search in Rome's sewer*
ē Cloācā Maximā cadunt *they fall out of Rome's sewer*
Cloācam Maximam *Cloaca Maxima*
īte ad Cloācam Maximam! *Go to Rome's sewer!*
in Cloācam Maximam iacite! *Throw into Rome's sewer!*
<u>**Crixaflamma**</u> *Crixaflamma, the best gladiator*
Crixaflammae *of Crixaflamma*
arma Crixaflammae *Crixaflamma's weapons*
scūtum Crixaflammae *Crixaflamma's shield*
Crixaflammam *Crixaflamma*
ad Crixaflammam iacit *throws towards Crixaflamma*
vult Crixaflammam esse... *wants Crixaflamma to be...*
<u>**diē**</u> *day*
diē Martis *on the day of Mars (Tuesday)*
diem *day*
diem Mārtis exspectat *waits for the day of Mars (Tuesday)*
diēs *day*

diēs Mārtis *day of Mars (Tuesday)*
diēs Sāturnī *day of Saturn (Saturday)*
diēs Veneris *day of Venus (Friday)*

E

ē/ex *of, out of, outside of*
    esse ex *to be outside of*
    cadunt ē *they fall out of*
    īre ē/ex *to go out of*
eāmus *Let's go!*
    ad lūdum eāmus! *Let's go to the gladiator school!*
  eō *I go*
    ad Forum Rōmānum eō *I'm going to the Roman Forum*
eī *to her/him*
    eī placēre *to be pleasing to her/him (s/he likes)*
erant *(more than one) were*
    in Amphitheātrō Flāviō erant *were in the Colosseum*
    in Cloācā Maximā erant *were in Rome's sewer*
ergō *therefore, so*
erit *will be*
    pugna erit *there will be a fight*
    laetus erit *will be happy*
  erō *I will be*
    laetus erō *I will be happy*
es *you are*
    optimus es *you are the best*
    bonus es *you are good*
    amīcus es *you are a friend*
    es sordidus *you are dirty*
    es malus *you are bad*
  esse *to be*
    vult Crixaflammam esse... *wants Crixaflamma to be...*
  est *is*
    est Rūfus *it's Rufus*
et *and*
eunt *they go*
    gladiātōrēs eunt *gladiators go*
  euntne? *Are they going?*
    euntne gladiātōrēs? *Are the gladiators going?*
exspectābat *was expecting, was waiting*

pugnam exspectābat *was waiting for a fight*
exspectant *(more than one) expect, wait for*
gladiātōrem exspectant *they wait for the gladiator*
exspectat *expects, waits for*
diem Mārtis exspectat *waits for the day of Mars (Tuesday)*
pugnam exspectat *waits for the fight*

F, G

Forō Rōmānō *Forum, Rome's marketplace*
in Forō esse *to be in the Roman Forum*
Forum Rōmānum *Roman Forum*
ad Forum Rōmānum it *goes to the Roman Forum*
frāter *brother*
frāter est Pīsō *the brother is Piso*
frātrem *brother*
frātrem habet *has a brother*
in frātrem pugnat *fights against brother*
frātrī *brother*
frātrī nōn placent *brother doesn't like (more than one)*
fūfae! *Gross!*
gladiātor *gladiator*
gladiātor nōn est *isn't a gladiator*
gladiātōrem *gladiator*
in gladiātōrem alium cadit *falls into another gladiator*
gladiātōrem exspectāre *to wait for a gladiator*
in gladiātōrem pugnat *fights against the gladiator*
gladiātōrem iacere *to throw a gladiator*
gladiātōrēs *gladiators*
gladiātōrēs eī placent *he likes gladiators*
gladiātōrēs pugnant *gladiators fight*
gladiātōrēs cadunt *the gladiators fall*
gladiātōrēs iacit *throws gladiators*
gladiōs *swords*
gladiōs habent *they have swords*
gladium *sword*
gladium habet *has a sword*
gladium iacit *throws the sword*

H, I

habē! *Have!*
>> habē gladium! *Have the sword!*
>> habē scūtum! *Have the shield!*
>> habē lūdum! *Have the gladiator school!*
> **habēbat** *had*
>> arma habēbat *had weapons*
> **habent** *(more than one) have*
>> multa arma habent *they have many weapons*
> **habeō** *I have*
>> arma iam nōn habeō *now I don't have the weapons*
> **habēre** *to have*
>> volō Oenobatiātum habēre... *I want Oenobatiatus to have...*
> **habēs** *have*
>> habēs arma *you have the weapons*
> **habet** *has*
>> frātrem habet *has a brother*
>> Quis arma habet? *Who has the weapons?*
>> lūdum habet *has a gladiator school*

iacere *to throw*
>> iacere vult *wants to throw*
> **iacit** *throws*
>> iacit ad *throws towards*
>> gladiātōrem iacit *throws a gladiator*
>> iacit in *throws into*
>> arma iacit *throws weapons*
> **iacite!** *Throw!*
>> in Cloācam Maximam iacite! *Throw into Rome's sewer!*
> **iaciunt** *(more than one) throw*
>> gladiātōrēs iaciunt *they throw the gladiators*

iam *now*

ībant *(more than one) were going*
>> ad lūdum ībant *they were going to the gladiator school*

iēcit *threw*
>> gladiātōrem iēcit *threw a gladiator*

in *in, into, on, against, onto*
>> in frātrem pugnat *fights against brother*
>> in Amphitheātrō Flāviō pugnāre *to fight in the Colosseum*
>> in Amphitheātrum Flāvium it *goes into the Colosseum*
>> in gladiātōrem alium cadit *falls into another gladiator*

cadit in *falls onto*
iacit in *throws into*

ineptissimus *most inept (unskilled, clumsy)*
    gladiātōr ineptissimus *the most unskilled gladiator*
  ineptior *more inept*
    gladiātōr ineptior *a clumsier gladiator*
  ineptōs *(more than one) inept*
    gladiātōrēs ineptōs *clumsy gladiators*
  ineptus *inept*
    gladiātor ineptus *clumsy gladiator*
    sum ineptus *I'm inept*

īrātissimus *very angry*
    īrātissimus esse *to be very angry*
  īrātior *angrier*
    gladiātōr īrātior *angrier gladiator*
  īrātum *angry*
    gladiātōrem īrātum *angry gladiator*
  īrātus *angry*
    īrātus est *is angry*

īre *to go*
    vīsne īre ad...? *Do you want to go to...?*
    īre mihi nōn placet *I don't like to go*
    īre volō *I want to go*
  it *goes*
    it ad *goes to*
    it in *goes into*
    it ē/ex *goes out of*
  īte *(more than one) Go!*
    īte ad! *Go to!*

L

laetī *happy (more than one)*
    laetī sunt *are happy*
  laetum *happy*
    vult esse laetum *wants to be happy*
  laetus *happy*
    laetus erit *will be happy*
    laetus erō *I will be happy*
lanista *gladiator trainer*
    sum lanista *I'm a gladiator trainer*

"lanista male..." "O, bad gladiator trainer..."

lanistae *of the gladiator trainer*
in lūdō lanistae *in the gladiator trainer's gladiator school*
lanistae malī *of the bad gladiator trainer*

lanistam *gladiator trainer*
lanistam habet *has a gladiator trainer*
lanistam iacere vult *wants to throw the gladiator trainer*
ad lanistam it *goes towards the gladiator trainer*

lūdō *gladiator school*
in lūdō lanistae *in the gladiator trainer's gladiator school*
in lūdō esse *to be in the gladiator school*

lūdum *gladiator school*
īte ad lūdum! *Go to the gladiator school!*
ad lūdum ībant *they were going to the gladiator school*
in lūdum it *goes into the gladiator school*
habēre lūdum *to have a gladiator school*

lūdus *gladiator school*
lūdus malus est *the gladiator school is bad*
lūdus lanistae malī *bad gladiator trainer's gladiator school*
lūdus Oenobatiātī *Oenobatiatus' gladiator school*

M

magna *big, great (more than one)*
arma magna *big weapons*
scūta magna *big shields*

magnī *big (more than one)*
gladiātōrēs magnī *big gladiators*

magnōs *big (more than one)*
gladiōs magnōs *big swords*

magnum *big*
gladium magnum *big sword*
scūtum magnum *big shield*

mala *bad (more than one)*
mala arma *bad weapons*

male *badly, bad*
male olēs! *you smell bad!*
nōn male oleō! *I don't smell bad!*
male pugnāre *to fight badly*
"lanista male..." "O, bad gladiator trainer..."

malī *of the bad*

lanistae malī *of the bad gladiator trainer*
malī *bad (more than one)*
   malī gladiātōrēs *bad gladiators*
malō *bad*
   in lūdō malō *in the bad gladiator school*
malōs *bad (more than one)*
   gladiātōrēs malōs *bad gladiators*
malum *bad*
   gladiātor malum *bad gladiator*
   lanistam malum *bad gladiator trainer*
malus *bad*
   gladiātor malus *bad gladiator*
   lūdus malus *bad gladiator school*
   lanista malus *bad gladiator trainer*
mihi *to/for me, my*
   mihi nōn placēre *I don't like*
multa *many*
   multa arma *many weapons*
multī *many*
   multī gladiātōrēs *many gladiators*
multōs *many*
   gladiātōrēs multōs *many gladiators*

N, O

nēscīmus *we don't know*
   nēsciō *I don't know*
   nēsciō-cūius *I-don't-know-whose (i.e. of Mr. no-name)*
      in lūdō nēsciō-cūius *in Mr. no-name's gladiator school*
   nēsciō-quem *I-don't-know-who (i.e. Mr. no-name)*
      nēsciō-quem gladiātōrem iēcit *threw Mr. no-name gladiator*
   nēsciō-quis *I-don't-know-who (i.e. Mr. no-name)*
      nēsciō-quis gladiātor *Mr. no-name gladiator*
nōn *not, does not*
Oenobatiāte *Oenobatiatus, Crixaflamma's gladiator trainer*
   "Oenobatiāte..." *"O Oenobatiatus..."*
   Oenobatiātī *of Oenobatiatus*
      in lūdō Oenobatiātī *in Oenobatiatus' gladiator school*
   Oenobatiātus *Oenobatiatus*
      Oenobatiātus laetus est *Oenobatiatus is happy*

olēmus *we smell*
    male olēmus *we smell bad*
olent *(more than one) smell*
    male olent *they smell bad*
oleō *I smell*
    nōn male oleō! *I don't smell bad!*
olēs *you smell*
    male olēs! *you smell bad!*
olet *smells*
    Quis male olet? *Who smells bad?*
    bene olet *smells good*
optima *best (more than one)*
    optima sunt *are the best*
    arma optima *the best weapons*
optimē! *Great! Well done!*
    "optimē, Rūfe!" *"Great, Rufus!"*
optimum *best*
    gladiātōrem optimum *the best gladiator*
    lanistam optimum *the best gladiator trainer*
    scūtum optimum *the best shield*
optimus *best*
    gladiātor optimus *the best gladiator*
    lanista optimus *the best gladiator trainer*
    lūdus optimus *the best gladiator school*

P

parva *small (more than one)*
    arma parva *small weapons*
    scūta parva *small shields*
parvī *small (more than one)*
    gladiātōrēs parvī *small gladiators*
parvissimus *very small*
    scūtum parvissimum *very small shield*
parvōs *small (more than one)*
    gladiōs parvōs *small swords*
parvum *small*
    gladium parvum *small sword*
Pīsō *Piso, Rūfus' brother*
    frāter est Pīsō *the brother is Piso*
Pīsōnem *Piso*

69

in frātrem, Pīsōnem, pugnat *fights against brother, Piso*

Pīsōnī *Piso*
    Pīsōnī nōn placet *Piso doesn't like*

placent *like (more than one thing)*
    eī placent *likes*
    Rūfō placent *Rufus likes*
    frātrī nōn placent *brother doesn't like*
    mihi nōn placent *I don't like*

placet *like*
    mihi nōn placet *I don't like*
    Pīsōnī nōn placet *Piso doesn't like*

pugna *a fight*
    pugna erit *there will be a fight*

pugnā! *Fight!*
    pugnā, Crixaflamma! *Fight, Crixaflamma!*

pugnābit *will fight*
    gladiātor pugnābit *the gladiator will fight*

pugnābunt *(more than one) will fight*
    diē Martis pugnābunt *will fight on the day of Mars (Tuesday)*

pugnam *a fight*
    pugnam bonam *good fight*

pugnant *(more than one) fight*
    gladiātōrēs pugnant *gladiators fight*

pugnat *fights*
    in frātrem pugnat *fights against brother*
    in gladiātōrēs pugnat *fights against gladiators*

pugnem *I might fight*
    Quōmodō pugnem? *How am I supposed to fight?*

Q

quaeram *I will search for*
    arma quaeram *I will searches for the weapons*

quaerāmus! *Let's search!*
    arma quaerāmus! *Let's search for the weapons!*

quaere! *Search!*
    arma quaere! *Search for the weapons!*

quaerere *to search*
    vīsne arma quaerere *Do you want to search for weapons?*

quaerite! *(more than one) Search!*
    gladiātōrēs, arma quaerite! *Gladiators, search for weapons!*

quaerit *searches for*
    gladium quaerit *searches for a sword*
    quoque quaerit *also searches*
quaerunt *(more than one) search*
    quaerunt in *they search in*
quoque *also*
Quis? *Who?*
Quōmodō? *How?*

R, S

Rōmae *Rome*
    est Rōmae *is in Rome*
Rōmānī *Romans*
    Rōmānī exspectant *the Romans wait*
    multī Rōmānī *many Romans*
Rūfe *Rufus, our Roman boy*
    "Rūfe,..." *"O Rufus,..."*
  Rūfō *Rufus*
    Rūfō placent *Rufus likes*
  Rūfum *Rufus*
    ad Rūfum it *goes to Rufus*
    Rūfum iacere vult *wants to throw Rufus*
  Rūfus *Rufus*
    est Rūfus *it's Rufus*
scūta *shields*
    scūta habent *they have shields*
  scūtum *shield*
    ad scūtum iacit *throws towards the shield*
    scūtum Crixaflammae *Crixaflamma's shield*
    in scūtum cadit *falls onto a shield*
    super scūtum *on top of the shield*
sed *but*
sordida *dirty*
    Cloāca Maxima sordida est *Rome's sewer is dirty*
  sordidī *(more than one) dirty*
    gladiātōrēs sordidī sunt *gladiators are dirty*
    sordidī sumus *we are dirty*
  sordidus *dirty*
    sordidus esse *to be dirty*
subitō *suddenly*

sum *I am*
>> sum lanista *I'm a gladiator trainer*
>> amīcus sum *I'm a friend*
>> īrātissimus sum *I'm very angry*
> **sumus** *we are*
>> sordidī sumus *we are dirty*
> **sunt** *(more than one) are*
>> multī sunt *there are many*
>> optima sunt *they are the best*
>> laetī sunt *they are happy*
>> sunt in *they are in*
>> sordidī sunt *they are dirty*
> **suntne?** *Are they?*
>> suntne in Forō Rōmānō *Are they in the Roman Forum?*

super *after, on top of*
>> super alium alius *one after another*
>> super scūtum *on top of the shield*

U, V

Ubi? *Where?*

valdē *really, very*

vīsne? *Do you want?*
>> vīsne īre? *Do you want to go?*
>> vīsne quaerere? *Do you want to search?*

volō *I want*
>> īre volō *I want to go*
>> arma quoque volō *I also want the weapons*
>> volō Oenobatiātum habēre... *I want Oenobatiatus to have...*

vult *wants*
>> arma vult *wants weapons*
>> vult Crixaflammam esse... *wants Crixaflamma to be...*
>> iacere vult *wants to throw*

Pisoverse Novellas & Resources

Magister P's Pop-Up Grammar

Pop-Up Grammar occurs when a student—not teacher—asks about a particular language feature, and the teacher offers a very brief explanation in order to continue communicating (i.e. interpreting, negotiating, and expressing meaning during reading or interacting).

Teachers can use this resource to provide such explanations, or students can keep this resource handy for reference when the teacher is unavailable. Characters and details from the Pisoverse novellas are used as examples of the most common of common Latin grammar.

> MAGISTER P's
> POP-UP GRAMMAR
> A "QUICK" REFERENCE
>
> Satisfying one's curiosity
> about common features of Latin
> in a comprehensible way
>
> BY LANCE PIANTAGGINI

Level AA
Early Beginner

Mārcus magulus
(11 cognates + 8 other words)

Marcus likes being a young Roman mage, but such a conspicuous combo presents problems in Egypt after he and his parents relocate from Rome. Despite generously offering his magical talents, this young mage feels like an obvious outsider, sometimes wishing he were invisible. Have you ever felt that way? Marcus searches Egypt for a place to be openly accepted, and even has a run-in with the famously fiendish Sphinx! Can Marcus escape unscathed?

Olianna et obiectum magicum
(12 cognates + 12 other words)

Olianna is different from the rest of her family, and finds herself excluded as a result. Have you ever felt that way? One day, a magical object appears that just might change everything for good. However, will it really be for the better? Can you spot any morals in this tale told from different perspectives?

a Latin Novella by Lance Piantaggini

Rūfus lutulentus
(20 words)

Was there a time when you or your younger siblings went through some kind of gross phase? Rufus is a Roman boy who likes to be muddy. He wants to be covered in mud everywhere in Rome, but quickly learns from Romans who bathe daily that it's not OK to do so in public. Can Rufus find a way to be muddy?

Rūfus et Lūcia: līberī lutulentī
(25-70 words)

Lucia, of Arianne Belzer's Lūcia: puella mala, joins Rufus in this collection of 18 additional stories. This muddy duo has fun in the second of each chapter expansion. Use to provide more exposure to words from the novella, or as a Free Voluntary Reading (FVR) option for all students, independent from Rūfus lutulentus.

Quīntus et nox horrifica
(26 cognates, 26 other words)

Monsters and ghosts...could they be real?! Is YOUR house haunted? Have YOU ever seen a ghost? Quintus is home alone when things start to go bump in the night in this scary novella. It works well with any Roman House unit, and would be a quick read for anyone interested in Pliny's ghost story.

Syra sōla
(29 words)

Syra likes being alone, but there are too many people everywhere in Rome! Taking her friend's advice, Syra travels to the famous coastal towns of Pompeii and Herculaneum in search of solitude. Can she find it?

Syra et animālia
(35-85 words)

In this collection of 20 additional stories, Syra encounters animals around Rome. Use to provide more exposure to words from the novella, or as a Free Voluntary Reading (FVR) option for all students, independent from Syra sōla.

Poenica purpurāria
(16 cognates, 19 other words)

Poenica is an immigrant from Tyre, the Phoenician city known for its purple. She's an extraordinary purple-dyer who wants to become a tightrope walker! In this tale, her shop is visited by different Romans looking to get togas purpled, as well as an honored Vestal in need of a new trim on her sacred veil. Some requests are realistic—others ridiculous. Is life all work and no play? Can Poenica find the time to tightrope walk?

Olianna et sandalia extraōrdināria
(20 cognates, 20 other words)

Olianna learns more about herself and her family in this psychological thriller continuation of "Olianna et obiectum magicum." We begin at a critical moment in the original, yet in this new tale, not only does the magical object appear to Olianna, but so do a pair of extraordinary sandals! Olianna has some choices to make. How will her decisions affect the timeline? Will things ever get back to normal? If so, is that for the better, or worse?

Pīsō perturbātus
(36 words)

Piso minds his Ps and Qs..(and Cs...and Ns and Os) in this alliterative tongue-twisting tale touching upon the Roman concepts of ōtium and negōtium. Before Piso becomes a little poet, early signs of an old curmudgeon can be seen.

Drūsilla in Subūrā
(38 words)

Drusilla is a Roman girl who loves to eat, but doesn't know how precious her favorite foods are. In this tale featuring all kinds of Romans living within, and beyond their means, will Drusilla discover how fortunate she is?

Rūfus et arma ātra
(40 words)

Rufus is a Roman boy who excitedly awaits an upcoming fight featuring the best gladiator, Crixaflamma. After a victorious gladiatorial combat in the Flavian Amphitheater (i.e. Colosseum), Crixaflamma's weapons suddenly go missing! Can Rufus help find the missing weapons?

Rūfus et gladiātōrēs
(49-104 words)

This collection of 28 stories adds details to characters and events from Rūfus et arma ātra, as well as additional, new cultural information about Rome, and gladiators. Use to provide more exposure to words from the novella, or as a Free Voluntary Reading (FVR) option for all students, independent from Rūfus et arma ātra.

Level A
Beginner

Mārcus et scytala Caesaris
(20 cognates + 30 other words)

Marcus has lost something valuable containing a secret message that once belonged to Julius Caesar. Even worse, it was passed down to Marcus' father for safekeeping, and he doesn't know it's missing! As Marcus and his friend Soeris search Alexandria for clues of its whereabouts, hieroglyphs keep appearing magically. Yet, are they to help, or hinder? Can Marcus decipher the hieroglyphs with Soeris' help, and find Caesar's secret message?

Agrippīna aurīga

Agrippīna aurīga
(24 cognates + 33 other words)

Young Agrippina wants to race chariots, but a small girl from Lusitania couldn't possibly do that...could she?! After a victorious race in the stadium of Emerita, the local crowd favorite charioteer, Gaius Appuleius Dicloes, runs into trouble, and it's up to Agrippina to step into much bigger shoes. Can she take on the reins in this equine escapade?

diāria sīderum
(30-60 cognates + 50-100 other words)

Not much was known about The Architects— guardians of the stars—until their diaries were found in dark caves sometime in the Tenth Age. Explore their mysterious observations from the Seventh Age (after the Necessary Conflict), a time just before all evidence of their existence vanished for millenia! What happened to The Architects? Can you reconstruct the events that led to the disappearance of this ancient culture?

trēs amīcī
et mōnstrum saevum

trēs amīcī et mōnstrum saevum
(28 cognates + 59 other words)

What became of the quest that Quintus' mother entrusted to Sextus and Syra in Drūsilla et convīvium magārum? Quintus finds himself alone in a dark wood (or so he thinks). Divine intervention is needed to keep Quintus safe, but can the gods overcome an ancient evil spurred on by Juno's wrath? How can Quintus' friends help?

sitne amor?
(36 cognates, 53 other words)

Piso and Syra are friends, but is it more than that? Sextus and his non-binary friend, Valens, help Piso understand his new feelings, how to express them, and how NOT to express them! This is a story of desire, and discovery. Could it be love?

ecce, poēmata discipulīs
(77 cognates + 121 other words)

"Wait, we have to read...Eutropius...who's that?! Homework on a Friday?! Class for an hour straight without a break?! Oh no, more tests in Math?! What, no glossary?! Why can't we just read?! Honestly, I was in bed (but the teacher doesn't know!)..." This collection of 33 poems is a humorous yet honest reflection of school, Latin class, homework, tests, Romans, teaching, and remote learning.

Magister P's Poetry Practice

Ain't got rhythm? This book can help. You'll be presented with a rhythm and two words, phrases, or patterns, one of which matches. There are three levels, Noob, Confident, and Boss, with a total of 328 practice. This book draws its words, phrases, and patterns entirely from "ecce, poemata discipulis!," the book of poetry with over 270 lines of dactylic hexameter. Perhaps a first of its kind, too, this book can be used by students and their teacher at the same time. Therefore, consider this book a resource for going on a rhythmic journey together.

Agrippīna: māter fortis
(65 words)

Agrippīna is the mother of Rūfus and Pīsō. She wears dresses and prepares dinner like other Roman mothers, but she has a secret—she is strong, likes wearing armor, and can fight just like her husband! Can she keep this secret from her family and friends?

Līvia: māter ēloquens
(44-86 words)

Livia is the mother of Drusilla and Sextus. She wears dresses and prepares dinner like other Roman mothers, but she has a secret—she is well-spoken, likes wearing togas, and practices public speaking just like her brother, Gaius! Can she keep this secret from her family and friends? Livia: mater eloquens includes 3 versions under one cover. The first level, (Alpha), is simpler than Agrippina: mater fortis; the second level, (Beta) is the same level, and the third, (Gamma-Delta) is more complex.

Pīsō et Syra et pōtiōnēs mysticae
(163 cognates, 7 other words)
Piso can't seem to write any poetry. He's distracted, and can't sleep. What's going on?! Is he sick?! Is it anxiety?! On Syra's advice, Piso seeks mystical remedies that have very—different—effects. Can he persevere?

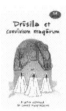

Drūsilla et convīvim magārum
(58 words)
Drusilla lives next to Piso. Like many Romans, she likes to eat, especially peacocks! As the Roman army returns, she awaits a big dinner party celebrating the return of her father, Julius. One day, however, she sees a suspicious figure give something to her brother. Who was it? Is her brother in danger? Is she in danger?

Level B
Advanced Beginner

mȳthos malus: convīvium Terregis
(41 cognates + 56 other words)
An obvious nod to Petronius' Cena Trimalchionis, yes, but this is not an adaptation, by any means. In this tale, Terrex can't get anything right during his latest dinner party. He's confused about Catullus' carmina, and says silly things left and right as his guests do all they can to be polite, though patience is running low. With guests even fact-checking amongst themselves, can Terrex say something remotely close to being true? Will the guests mind their manners and escape without offending their host?

sīgna zōdiaca Vol. 1
(63 cognates, 84 other words)
sīgna zōdiaca Vol. 2
(63 cognates, 92 other words)
sīgna zōdiaca Vol. 3
(62 cognates, 93 other words)

Do you like stories about gods and monsters? Did you know that the zodiac signs are based on Greek and Roman mythology? Your zodiac sign can tell you a lot about yourself, but not everyone feels that strong connection. Are your qualities different from your sign? Are they the same? Read signa zodiaca to find out! These readers are part non-fiction, and part Classical adaptation, providing information about the zodiac signs as well as two tiered versions of associated myths.

Level C
Low Intermediate

fragmenta Pīsōnis
(96 words)

This collection of poetry is inspired by scenes and characters from the Pisoverse, and features 50 new lines of poetry in dactylic hexameter, hendecasyllables, and scazon (i.e. limping iambics)! fragmenta Pīsōnis can be used as a transition to the Piso Ille Poetulus novella, or as additional reading for students comfortable with poetry having read the novella already.

Pīsō Ille Poētulus
(108 words)

Piso is a Roman boy who wants to be a great poet like Virgil. His family, however, wants him to be a soldier like his father. Can Piso convince his family that poetry is a worthwhile profession? Features 22 original, new lines of dactylic hexameter.

Pīsō: Tiered Versions
(68-138 words)

This novella combines features of Livia: mater eloquens with the tiered versions of the Piso Ille Poetulus story taken from its Teacher's Guide and Student Workbook. There are 4 different levels under one cover, which readers choose, switching between them at any time. Piso: Tiered Versions could be used as scaffolding for reading the original novella, Piso Ille Poetulus. Alternatively, it could be read independently as a Free Voluntary Reading (FVR) option, leaving it up to the learner which level to read.

Tiberius et Gallisēna ultima
(155 words)

Tiberius is on the run. Fleeing from an attacking Germanic tribe, the soldier finds himself separated from the Roman army. Trying to escape Gaul, he gets help from an unexpected source—a magical druid priestess (a "Gaul" in his language, "Celt" in hers). With her help, can Tiberius survive the punishing landscape of Gaul with the Germanic tribe in pursuit, and make his way home to see Rufus, Piso, and Agrippina once again?

...and more!
See magisterp.com for the latest:

teacher's materials
other books
audio

Made in the USA
Columbia, SC
02 September 2022

66536846R00050